We hope you enjoy our Abbey Heroes and Villains book. Monks and nuns enjoyed a relatively secure life, tucked away in stunning abbeys, in some of the most beautiful areas in Britain. However, once Henry VIII decided that they had too much wealth and power, their fate was sealed. Today our ruined abbeys offer us a taste of what life was like living and working in a community dedicated to prayer and hard work.

Colour, keep and learn as you read through this fascinating activity book.

Contents

	page
Monastic Orders in Britain	3
Who Joined a Monastery?	4
The Holy Orders	5
Land and Wealth	7
Work, Education and Music	8
A Day in the life of Brother Egbert	9
Life in a Monastery	11
Abbey Histories Including:	13
Mount Grace Priory	
Fountains Abbey	
Battle Abbey	
Whitby Abbey	
Jedburgh Abbey	
Glastonbury Abbey	
Llanthony Priory	
Lindisfarne Priory	
Dissolution of the Monasteries	19
Quiz	21
Map	22

Written and illustrated by Les Ives
Researched by Helen Childs

Published by Colour History Ltd ©2005

Monastic Orders in Britain

The first known monasteries were built in the Middle East in the 3rd century AD. As Christianity spread across Europe, monasteries were built and communities of monks and nuns were established to run them.

As we will discover, monastic orders were many and varied, but the one common link they all observed was the Rule of St Benedict. In 6th century Italy in the monastery of Monte Cassino, Benedict outlined his guide to the spiritual daily life for men and women running the monasteries of Europe and beyond.

Based upon communal living, monks and nuns shared a similar life style. They slept in dormitories, ate and prayed together. It was a life without privacy, or any form of personal possessions. Cleanliness and good manners were as highly regarded as keeping the soul and the body clean and healthy. The day was an orderly succession of prayer, hard work and a strictly controlled diet.

Education and learning were an important part of monastic life. The writing of books, reading and running schools, helped to spread Christianity in the pagan lands of Dark Age Europe. Usually self-sufficient, they were able to provide food and medicines for the communities they lived in. They often provided a safe haven for criminals if they managed to reach the sanctuary of the monastery gates.

By the 12th century, monasteries were established throughout Europe. They had nearly developed into self-contained towns, exerting great influence in all areas of local life. Owning vast estates, they provided prosperity and employment for local communities and boosted the economy of the countries they lived in. In England it was their independence and wealth, which finally brought about their downfall.

Monasteries in Britain

In the 5th century St Patrick brought Christianity to Ireland. His followers travelled to England and spread Celtic Christianity in the north, whilst St Augustine spread the Roman mission in the south. Disrupted firstly by Anglo-Saxon and then Viking raiders, Christian influence struggled during the 9th and 10th centuries. The Norman Conquest of 1066 re-established monastic orders in Britain, even surviving the ravages of the Black Death, and it continued until the dissolution of the mid 16th century.

Viking attack!

Who Joined a Monastery?

Although open to everyone, men and women entering a monastery, or convent were expected to provide a small endowment of land. This meant that most orders consisted of members from well off families. Poorer people could enter as lay brothers, or sisters providing labour instead of land.

Some children were given away to monasteries, and older people were also accepted. It was a life of spiritual discipline and hard work, but it was a secure life, free from famine and bloodshed. Females entering a convent could escape the dangers of childbirth, which was a common cause of early death in females at this time.

Did you know!

It wasn't until the 12th century that the practice of "giving away" your children to the church became unfashionable.

Monks and nuns owned nothing - not even their habit!

Monks had their heads shaved once every three weeks. Shaving went in order of seniority, so when it came to the turn of the novice monks, the towels were soaking wet and the razors were blunt!

Training

It was common in an average land owning family of medieval Britain, for the eldest son to inherit the land, whilst the second son would enter the church.

Educated at home by the local priest, the child would be taught Latin and the scriptures. At about eight years of age, he would be taken to the monastery and given to the monks. A sum of money, or endowment of land would also be handed over. By doing this people believed that spiritually they were helping their family's future, in this life and the next.

In a more practical way they were ensuring that their children received an education. Schools in medieval Britain were rare and monks and nuns were the most educated people of the middle ages. In many regions of the country they were the only educated people!

Situated on the western side of the monastery in the cloisters daily classes were conducted by the novice master, or mistress for nuns. A variety of lessons would be taught and the young pupils were instructed in the traditions of monastic life. Pupils took part in services and religious ceremonies.

After making their first vows, the boys would receive their "tonsure," the monk's distinctive haircut. As the boy grew into his teens he would make his final vows of poverty, chastity and obedience. Once these were made the young man had become a monk.

Children were given away to monasteries

The Holy Orders

The Benedictines

St Augustine established the first Benedictine monastery at Canterbury in 597 AD. The black robed monks were the original order of monks in Britain and they ran many of the most powerful and wealthiest monasteries. St Dunstan, the famous abbot of Glastonbury, expanded the order after the Viking wars of the 9th century and by 1066 there were over three dozen Benedictine houses in England. During the 10th century, the order was accused of laziness and failing the strict rules of St Benedict. As a result other religious groups arrived from Europe. However, the order continued to grow and by the time of the dissolution, there were 136 Benedictine houses throughout Britain.

The Cluniacs

The Cluniacs originated from the famous Cluny Abbey in France and wanted to restore the strict Benedictine way of life. It was a very centralised order, with the Abbot of Cluny controlling all Cluniac institutions. Arriving in England at Lewes in 1078, Cluniac establishments, known as priories, were smaller than their Benedictine counterparts, but their services and vestments were much grander. Putting prayer and study before any form of manual labour, they used paid servants to run their estates. The order had grown to 38 priories by the time of the dissolution.

Did you know!

Church leaders hand picked the Chaplains who conducted services to nuns in convents, choosing old and not very good looking ones. They were worried that nuns would gossip about younger priests!

Benedictine Monk **Cluniac Monk**

The Cistercians

Established in Citeaux in France, the first Cistercian monks arrived at Rievaulx in Yorkshire in 1131 AD. With an appetite for hard work and clad in their rough white wool habits, the order began to build their elegant, gothic style abbeys in remote and isolated locations. They were a forward thinking order and devised the system of lay brothers, who undertook much of the manual labour on their estates. With help from St Bernard, the famous Abbot of Clairvaux in France, the order gathered in strength, and by 1152 there were 54 Cistercian monasteries in England. Their success was due to their ownership and successful management of great estates of land. Abbeys such as Fountains, near Ripon were hugely important to the growth of the wool and cloth trade in Britain.

The Carthusians

They originated from Grande Chartreuse in France, the Carthusians were the strictest and most devout of all of the holy orders in Britain. Clad in coarse hair shirts, the Carthusians led a life of silence, prayer and fasting. Their monasteries consisted of single cells and small gardens, where the monks spent virtually their entire lives. Their fellow monks were only seen in chapel, or when eating on a Sunday, or feast days. They were totally isolated from the outside world. To exist as they did, the order had to be well organised. Lay brothers would do the manual labour required in the grounds and advanced sanitary systems gave them fresh water and good toilets. Less in number than other religious orders, examples of "charterhouses" exist at Mount Grace Priory in Yorkshire and Sheen in Surrey. Charterhouse School in London was the site of the main Carthusian Monastery in England.

Cistercian Monk

Carthusian Monk

Nun

Nuns

Women entering convents, or nunneries in medieval Britain had a similar daily routine to that of the monks. An Abbess was in overall charge with a Prioress her deputy. Officials would be appointed to run the infirmary, the kitchen and wine cellars. The Precentor taught music and singing, the Novice mistress educated the juniors. The Almoner gave gifts of money, food and clothes to the beggars who called. Lay sisters undertook the daily manual tasks, leaving the nuns to work and pray. One difference from their male counterparts was that having entered a nunnery, unless expelled, a nun would rarely if ever leave again. They were not as numerous as the monasteries, but there were about 150 nunneries by the time of the Black Death.

Canons and Friars

As the monastic communities attracted criticism in the 12th century for their wealth and isolation, Augustinian and Premonstratensian canons arrived in England. Establishing their houses near castles and towns, they helped to spread Christianity to the poor and also tended the sick. A century later, St Francis and St Dominic established the order of friars. Wandering the land they preached to all communities and proved very popular.

Land and Wealth

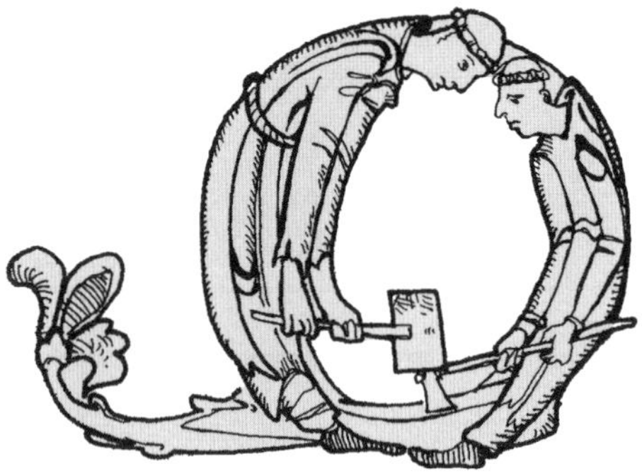

From very humble beginnings, many monastic institutions had acquired great wealth by the turn of the 12th century. But, how did they gain control and run their large estates?

The Norman Conquest of 1066 introduced the monastic ideals of Europe into the Christian church of Britain. Existing monasteries were enlarged and great cathedrals built, including Norwich, Durham and Winchester. Church courts were established and the rules of the Pope were adopted as law. Although newly appointed Norman abbots often caused resentment among the Saxon clergy; over time the church emerged stronger, with closer links to the kings and queens of Britain.

As the monasteries grew in size, they became focal points for people to visit. Royal parties and noblemen would come to the larger religious houses, often staying for weeks at a time. St Benedict instructed that everyone should be made welcome, and the patronage of the wealthy was good for the church. Large endowments of money and land were donated by the wealthy, in the hope of securing a safe passage in the after life!

As the estates grew large numbers of people were required to run them. Although some monks worked as farmers, their role gradually became more managerial rather than the physical labour. Lay brothers, who were less educated monks and worked in the fields with serfs. The serfs usually had houses on the land and had little choice, but to work for their new landlords. Much of the endowed property was miles away from the monasteries, so it was leased to farmers, creating good incomes from rent.

Within the monastery walls builders, gardeners, launderers and cooks were employed to ensure the smooth running of the establishment. This enabled the monks and nuns to concentrate on their priorities - prayer, work, education and medicine.

Serfs and lay brothers worked the land

Work, Education and Music

With so much of their life dedicated to worship in church, monks and nuns were at the forefront of medieval music. Many of the services were chanted rather than spoken. Worshippers would begin to chant words, followed by others, building mood like music, which became known as "plainsong." Members of the holy orders were trained to read music and soon they began to write their own hymns.

The work of the medieval monk has provided us with virtually all of our knowledge of life at that time. They wrote detailed accounts of every aspect of the medieval era. Working on parchment paper and writing with a quill, a monk could take years to produce one beautifully hand written and illustrated book. Unhindered by matters of profit and time, the books were often of exquisite quality.

Monks and Nuns provided schools for the local communities. The early monasteries concentrated on the education of novice clergy and the sons and daughters of local noblemen. As time progressed small schools were established in local villages and towns. Canons and travelling friars were responsible for most of the teaching.

Singing was an important part of daily life

The Precentor was responsible for teaching singing lessons and arranged the music for church services and religious festivals.

On special Saints day's plays based on stories from the bible would be presented and performed in front of local communities. With their involvement in both music and acting, the monks and nuns of medieval Britain did a great deal to establish what we now know as musical theatre.

The Venerable Bede
673 - 735

Having joined Jarrow Monastery at the age of seven, the Venerable Bede was England's best known monastic writer. He rarely travelled from his north east home, and he dedicated his life to writing. He wrote about subjects as diverse as mathematics, poetry and time keeping. His books are an important part of our current understanding of life in medieval Britain.

Did you know!

Stale urine was used to help make leather and also to dye wool!

Monks used soaked and stretched sheepskins to make the pages for their writing. To produce one bible required one whole flock of sheep!

A day in the life of Brother Egbert

Brother Egbert is a monk and lives in a medieval monastery. He has kindly taken the time to tell you about life in the monastery and his daily routine.

12th May 1236

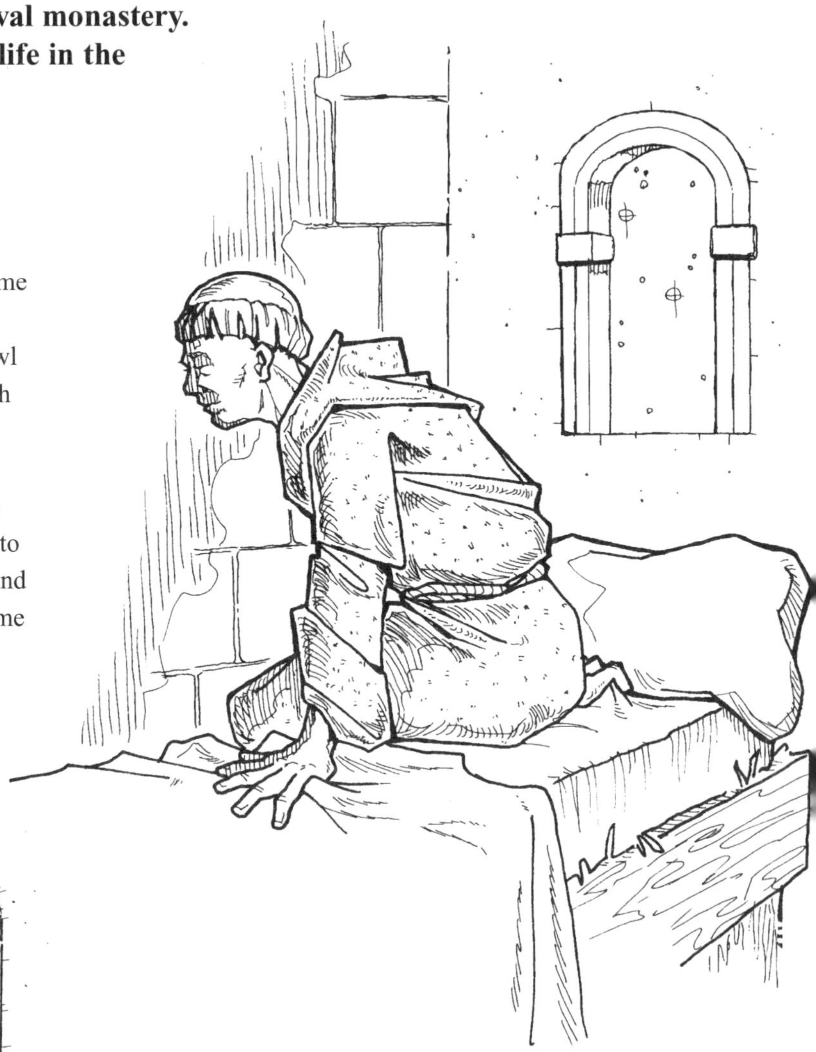

At midnight, with the sound of a ringing church bell it is time to get up. My day has begun. I climb out of my straw-lined bed, fully dressed in my habit. With only my shoes and cowl to put on, I quickly follow the procession of monks, through the dormitory door and down the night stairs to chapel for matins (meaning 'first'). This is where we all pray for one hour. We remain in the church for the second service of the day called Lauds meaning 'praise'. After prayer we return to our bed for a further five hours sleep. At 7 o'clock the sound of the ringing bell announces once more that it is time for me to return to the church for another half hour service before breakfast.

After this service some monks remain in the church to celebrate the first mass of the day. This is the most important service, where monks, servants and farmhands can attend. The monk's who are not attending mass, wash and change their clothes. We have a change of clothes once a week.

At 8 o'clock it is breakfast time when we receive bread and a cup of water, served in the refectory. At 8.30 am it is time for our second mass in the church, from there we will attend a chapter meeting in the Chapter House. Once we have assembled, the Abbot will enter the room and we rise to our feet, bowing our heads as a sign of respect, as he passes by.

Daily tasks are given out and brothers pass on and discuss news, ideas or plans for the monastery. Others speak of their sins and the Abbot listens and hands out punishments, according to the seriousness of the crime. After the meeting junior monks, known as novices, are allowed to walk and talk in the cloister.

Telling the time in a monastery is extremely important. We need to maintain the same cycle of prayer each day. We make sure that the whole community can gather 7 or 8 times for prayer and activities. To make this possible we use a water clock. This is a container which loses a set amount of water, during a given amount of time. It is the most accurate way to measure time in medieval Britain.

High mass is conducted at 10 o'clock. This is the most solemn service of the day where we sing hymns and chant. After the half hour service the senior monks of the monastery organise the servants and labourers on our farms.

At 11 o'clock it is time for our dinner. We live on a simple diet of bread, eggs, fruit and vegetables. Meat is only eaten to aid recovery from sickness. Watered down ale, or wine is drunk, although a brother once told me that some monks have fallen into the temptation of excessive drinking, resulting in drunken behaviour!

During our meal absolute silence is expected, so that readings from a religious text can be heard. After dinner old, or sickly monks are allowed to return to bed for an extra hour.

Between the hours of 12.30 pm and 5 o'clock, I work in the cloisters. I sit at my small wooden desk, and spend the afternoon copying religious texts onto sheets of parchment. I also spend time reading in the library. I am lucky to be educated, as my less capable lay brothers will be working long, hard days in the fields, or in the monastery herb gardens. At 5 o'clock we have vespers meaning 'evening' and collation, which means 'holy readings'. These are conducted in the church, and usually last for about an hour.

Supper is eaten in the refectory at 6 pm, after which we can relax in the cloister or gardens. During winter, if it is cold, we gather in the warming room, the only place in the monastery which has heating. At 7 o clock, the final prayers of the day are offered. These are known as 'compline', which means ending, this signals the end of the day. It is now time to retire to our dormitory to sleep until midnight, when our next day begins.

Did you know!

For misbehaving a monk could be flogged, or made to lie in the doorway of the chapel, for the other brothers to step over him!

Monks and nuns were very hygienic and kept themselves clean with regular washing. Unless you were ill baths were forbidden!

Life in a Monastery

The monasteries were an important part of medieval life in Britain. Usually self-sufficient in the production of food they owned great estates of land. They were places of religious importance, but played an important part in health, employment and economic prosperity.

1 CHAPEL

This was the most commonly used building in the monastery. The monks attended at least seven services a day where they would pray, sing and chant in continuous religious ritual. Standing for all of the services, their only rest was a kneeling stool known as a 'misericord'. Monks who dared to drift off to sleep had a lantern waved in their face to awaken them.

2 CLOISTER

The cloister was a covered walkway, which formed a square and surrounded a central lawn. Monks would read, write and study on the sunny western side of the cloister. Privacy and silence was strictly observed by the monks in their study. Larger monasteries had a well stocked library. The eastern side was used to train the novices in the rules and traditions of monastic life. The cloister was used for the three weekly ritual of head shaving, as well as the weekly ritual of washing their fellow monk's feet!

3 DORMITORY

All of the monks slept in a dormitory with only an Abbot or Abbess enjoying a separate room. The monks were required to sleep fully dressed, so that they could begin their work for God without delay. The monasteries had hygienic and advanced washing and toilet facilities.

4 INFIRMARY

Old and sick monks were treated in the infirmary. Monks were usually the best doctors of medieval times and they used herbs and spices to treat most ailments. Bleeding patients of blood was believed to cure sickness as wide ranging as toothache to liver problems! If a monk had been bled he could expect a few days rest from the rituals of monastic life. He may also enjoy a rare bath and a chance to gossip with his fellow patients.

5 HERB AND VEGETABLE GARDEN

Much of the work undertaken in the gardens, orchards and fields was performed by the lay brothers. Herbs from the herb garden were used for medicines to cure many ailments. Their knowledge and skill with herbal treatments was extensive

6 REFECTORY

Breakfast was taken in the late morning, and dinner and supper were the only other eating times. They would enter the refectory in an orderly file. The Abbot occupied the top table with the novice monks near to the door. To communicate in their silent meal, the monks used a complex sign language. Eating was a modest occasion and no one was permitted to leave the table until the meal was finished.

7 KITCHEN

The monk's diet consisted of bread, cheese, eggs, vegetables and fruit. Meat was only given to the sick. Watered down wine or beer was drunk. The larger monasteries had their own bakeries and brew houses. The diet was basic, but monks were at least free of the fear of famine, which gripped so many communities in medieval Britain.

8 CHAPTER HOUSE

The daily Chapter House meeting was held after morning mass. Overseen by the abbot, it was a way of ensuring that the rules of St Benedict were observed by all. After prayer and a reading from St Benedict's writings the daily tasks were issued. Outsiders were then asked to leave and private discussion took place about monastery affairs and the punishments to be given out to those whose standards had fallen.

Did you know!

Good table manners were very important in the refectory - even nuts had to be opened carefully with a knife!

The most unpopular job in a monastery? Solid waste was collected in a pit from under the monastery toilets, then put into barrows and used as manure!

Abbey Histories

Monasteries were particularly numerous in the early 14th century. There were as many as 500 scattered throughout Britain. Run by various monastic orders, they wielded great power and influence, second only to the crown. The Black Death of 1348 dealt a major blow to the numbers of monk's, and although many monasteries had recovered by the 1500's, none survived Henry VIII's dissolution.

Carthusian monk in his cell

Mount Grace Priory

The Priory was founded in 1398 by Thomas de Holand, the Duke of Surrey. It is one of only ten Carthusian charterhouses in England and was built specifically for the lifestyle of this solitary order of monks. Living in cells with their own gardens, the monks lived a hermit like existence, isolated from the outside world. The monks met with their brothers only to pray in church. They ate together on Sundays and weekly meetings were held in the Chapter House.

The austere nature of the order made it less popular than other medieval orders in Britain. The Black Death of 1348, which was so destructive for many of the population, increased the popularity of the Carthusians. The strict spiritual life the charterhouse monks led encouraged followers to believe that they would be protected from life's hardships.

As the order grew, building work continued at Mount Grace. A complex and advanced water system provided the monks with fresh water and good toilets. A lot of the estate work was undertaken by lay brothers and the efficient running of the Priory allowed the monks to concentrate on their study and prayer.

This solitary lifestyle was put under threat when the estate founder, de Holand, was executed for his part in a plot against King Henry IV. The Priory was handed over to the Augustinian canons at Guisbrough and the order's future looked bleak. However, the Prior, Henry Eccleston worked tirelessly to secure a lease on the site in 1508. Donations of money from wealthy benefactors and rents from land gave the Priory financial security. Unlike many monastic orders at the turn of the 16th century, there was a list of people waiting to join the monks of Mount Grace Priory.

The Carthusian order was at the forefront of opposition to Henry VIII's Act of Succession in 1534, legitimising the king's second marriage and the Act of Supremacy in 1535, when he became head of the English church. Carthusian charterhouse leaders were arrested and executed for their protest. In 1536 the king began his programme of dissolution and smaller religious houses were closed. Some church leaders backed the ill-fated "Pilgrimage of Grace" uprising. Prior Wilson at Mount Grace was wise enough not to involve himself with the rebels, but time was running out.

In 1539 larger monasteries were closed down and in December of that year, Prior Wilson and the 26 inhabitants of Mount Grace were pensioned off and the Priory was closed.

Mount Grace Priory

Fountains Abbey

Fountains Abbey, Britain's largest monastic ruin was established in 1132 AD. A group of thirteen monks had been expelled from St Mary's Abbey in York after religious differences, and they were given a site on the river Skell to re-establish themselves.

Described as "more fit for wild beasts than men to inhabit"- the area was rich in stone, timber and water. The industrious monks set about building their monastery. The early days were hard and it was not until the monks joined the Cistercian monastic order that their fortunes changed. St Bernard of Clairvaux, leader of the Cistercians, despatched monks to help with the construction and running of the new monastery.

Fountains Abbey

Less decorative than Benedictine monasteries, the architecture of Fountains was strong, its chapels and alters simple. The monks, clad in their habits of coarse un-dyed wool, entered the Cistercian routine with its strict daily programme of prayer, silence and meagre diet. However, the order introduced the system of lay brothers, where illiterate monks undertook a lot of the routine manual labour, required to run the monastery. Most importantly, they shepherded the vast flocks of sheep which lived in the huge estate's grounds.

By the middle of the 13th century, Fountains was a centre of great wealth and economic importance. Farming, lead and iron mining, quarrying and horse breeding added to the fortunes of the estate, which now stretched from Teeside to the Lake District.

The turn of the 14th century was a dark period for the Abbey. Continual border wars between Scotland and England resulted in Scottish raids and a succession of bad harvests weakened the power of Fountains. Worse was to come with the arrival of the Black Death. The terrible plague caused great loss of life among the valuable lay brothers, but by leasing out land to tenant farmers, the monastery regained a lot of its former power.

With Abbots in parliament, the future should have been secure, but the dissolution spared no one and in 1539, the great Yorkshire monastery was closed down.

Battle Abbey

On 14th October 1066 AD William, Duke of Normandy defeated English King Harold at the battle of Hastings. After the battle anyone carrying arms was massacred, but local people were shown leniency. However, on becoming king, William pursued and killed anyone who had fought against him. When the abbey building was proposed the Pope asked for it to be built at the site of the battle, as a memorial to those killed. He also instructed that the abbey's construction would serve as a penance for the needless bloodshed after the battle.

Battle Abbey

The king sent for Benedictine monks from Marmoutier Abbey in Normandy to begin the building work, but they were aghast when they saw the badly drained site. They attempted to move the building site, but the king was adamant and construction began in 1067 AD.

It took 9 years to complete the eastern arm, but the work was far from complete when William died in 1087. The king had been determined that the work would continue, and left his sword and coronation robes to the abbey. He decreed that all of the land and labour within one and a half miles belonged to the monks. With its financial status secure, the abbey church was consecrated in 1094 in the presence of William II, the Archbishop of Canterbury and seven Bishops.

The high alter of the church was erected near the spot where King Harold was thought to have fallen. The abbey was famous for the "Roll of Battle Abbey" - an inscription featuring the names of those who had fought for William, but it is now thought to be a forgery.

Over the next few years the abbey prospered from gifts of property, and it was now possible to buy large areas of land in the surrounding areas. The abbey's wealth and independence caused resentment and during the reigns of both Henry II and King John, the abbey had to fight to retain its royal status. Compromises were reached and the abbey continued to prosper with a large re-building programme, which continued throughout the 13th century.

Battle Abbey's fortunes finally changed after suffering repeated raids from France and in the early 14th century, many monks and labourers died from the Black Death. The Abbey had recovered financially by the turn of the following century, but Abbot John Hammond and his remaining 18 monks were forced to surrender to the crown in the dissolution on 27th May, 1538.

Whitby Abbey

Whitby Abbey was founded by St Hilda in 657 AD. She was an Anglo-Saxon woman who was educated in the court of King Edwin of Northumbria. Hilda established the abbey as a great place for spiritual education. Nuns and monks, landlords and kings, the wealthy and poor flocked to her monastery, where they could learn to read, write and study.

The Synod of 664 was held there, and the Christian church debated its future, whether to follow the Celtic, or the Roman teachings. Although Hilda was in favour of the Celtic church, the Roman mission was finally accepted. Suffering poor health in the last years of her life, Hilda died in 680, but the good work of the abbey continued. Caedmon regarded, as the first English Christian poet, studied within its walls and the fame of Whitby enabled it to become a royal burial ground.

The peace was brutally shattered in 867 AD when ferocious Viking raiders destroyed Whitby Abbey and the monks were forced to flee inland. So devastating was the destruction caused by the Danes that monastic life ceased to exist in Whitby, until the invasion of England by William of Normandy in 1066. The new Norman king revived monastic fortunes throughout Britain.

Ravaged by Vikings and soldiers of Henry VIII, Whitby Abbey was damaged be German Naval gunfire in World War I.

He ordered the building of imposing new cathedrals and old monasteries were repaired. His Benedictine Abbots modernised the English church. In 1073 one of William's knights, Reinfrid, visited the ruins of Whitby Abbey and was so inspired, that he converted to monastic life. Returning a few years later he restored the buildings to their former glory.

Reinfrid's Norman church could not cope with the number of pilgrims who travelled to Whitby. The massive project continued throughout the 13th and 14th centuries. Impressive as the buildings were, the abbey was in debt by the time the Black Death took its toll.

Many of the labourers died from the plague and the abbey found itself paying even more wages to the reduced labour force, whilst receiving less rental income from its tenants. The number of monks shrank from 40 to about half that number at the time of the dissolution. After escaping the first wave of closures, on 14th December 1539, Whitby Abbey was surrendered to the crown.

Whitby Abbey

Jedburgh Abbey

Situated on the north banks of the river Jed, Jedburgh Abbey was built in 1138 AD by King David I. The king was eager to demonstrate to his own people, as well as the English, that he could build a magnificent building to equal any in Britain.

Built of local stone it took over one hundred years to complete. The abbey was run by the Augustinian "black" Canons. Sadly, the abbey's completion coincided with the outbreak of the border wars between Scotland and England. Abbeys at Kelso, Melrose, Dryburgh and Jedburgh itself were regularly ransacked. Lead was taken from the roof to help construct English siege engines. As the opposing armies swept up and down the country, the monks lived in constant danger.

Jedburgh Abbey

It was the defeat of the Scottish army in 1547 by Henry VIII at the battle of Pinkie, which signalled the end of the abbey. As the English king continued his dissolution in England, Scotland undertook its own religious reformation. The power of the Catholic Church dwindled and by 1560, there were only eight Augustinian Canons left. They were left in peace to live out their lives in the remains of the embattled abbey.

Glastonbury Abbey

Glastonbury Abbey

In the 8th century Saxon King Ine built the first stone church here. The Christian site grew, but Danish raids on England caused it to fall into decay.

However, a young man called Dunstan, who had been educated at the abbey, was determined to restore it to its former glory. He introduced a new daily pattern of worship and work based upon the Rule written by St Benedict. Dunstan became so important that he was made Archbishop of Canterbury in 960 AD.

The Norman invasion of 1066 led to the construction of bigger, more beautiful abbey buildings. The first Abbot, Thurstin, appointed by the new king made many changes, which the monks did not like. A riot and bloodshed followed, but order was restored when a new Abbot was appointed. Disaster struck in 1184, when a terrible fire completely destroyed the abbey, but it was quickly rebuilt and grew rich with gifts from pilgrims and kings.

The Dissolution of the Monasteries brought a bloody end to Glastonbury Abbey. Although Henry VIII had closed almost all of the abbeys in England and Wales, Glastonbury's Abbot Whiting resisted him. The king accused him, falsely, of theft and treason and he was hanged with two of his monks. The abbey was then destroyed.

Llanthony Priory

In 1100 AD William de Lacy, a knight and relative of the Baron of Herefordshire, was out hunting when he came across the ruins of an ancient chapel. Believing it to have been the residence of St David, the young man became a hermit and lived amongst its crumbling walls. In time, he was joined by others. The Baron was so impressed by their spirit, living in this wild and inhospitable place, that he built a monastery on the site.

Llanthony Priory

Dedicated to John the Baptist, the monastery grew in size and importance. Its Augustinian Canons received royal patronage and guests from all over Britain, but problems lay ahead. The barren and rocky surroundings produced soil of poor quality for food and there were constant border wars. Raiding parties eventually forced the remaining 40 Canons to flee to Gloucester.

When peace returned to the area, the de Lacy family rebuilt the monastery, but its glory days were over. Owain Glyndwr's rebellion in the early 15th century caused more unrest and at the time of the dissolution, only four Canons lived at Llanthony.

Lindisfarne Priory

Lindisfarne Priory

In 635 AD St Aidan established the first simple monastery on the famous Holy Island of Lindisfarne. However, it was with the arrival of Cuthbert that the fame of this Christian site grew. Born the son of an Anglo-Saxon nobleman, Cuthbert left behind his life as a warrior and entered Melrose Abbey in 651.

He moved to Lindisfarne, where he became the Prior and his energy and enthusiasm greatly developed the island site. It grew in wealth and power and became a centre for pilgrims to visit. Shortly after his appointment as Bishop of Hexham, Cuthbert died and the famous Lindisfarne gospels were written in praise of his Sainthood. Sadly, the site's fame attracted the unwelcome attentions of the Vikings from Denmark. After ten decades of raids, robbery and bloodshed the monks finally abandoned the monastery and fled to Durham.

At the end of the 11th century, a band of monks returned to Holy Island and established the Priory again. Once the church was built, living quarters were added for the small group of monks who lived there. Fortifications were added in the following century, as the border wars with Scotland continued. Only half a dozen monks were thought to be in the Priory when it was forced to close in 1537 by Henry VIII.

Dissolution of the Monasteries

At the beginning of the 14th Century, the monastic way of life began to decline. Fewer people were joining the holy orders and as the Black Death ravaged the country in 1348 AD the numbers dwindled further. Many of the abbeys were only half full and some of the great buildings began to show signs of decay.

When Henry VIII came to the throne of England in 1509, it was the beginning of the end for the religious houses in Britain. King Henry's reasons for attacking the monasteries were varied. He had recently left the Catholic Church and joined the newly formed Church of England. He distrusted the old orders and saw them as a threat to his power and popularity. However, years of war with France had emptied the Crown's pockets and the church had a lot of what the king desired - land and money!

Henry envied the wealth of the monasteries

The Suppression Act of 1536 was introduced for small religious houses, so they could be taken over by the crown. The displaced occupants were given pensions, or employment elsewhere. The Act was seen as fair, which helped it to go through Parliament, but this was only the beginning.

Although only three out of every ten religious houses were closed in the early days of the Suppression Act, it caused a great deal of ill feeling. In the north of England a revolt known as the "Pilgrimage of Grace" took place. A group of Catholic noblemen had raised an army and demanded the return of all religious properties.

The revolt was disorganised and when the leaders began to fall out with each other, the rebellion ended without a war. The king's revenge was swift and brutal. Over 250 of the leaders and supporters of the failed revolt were executed and Henry now had the opportunity to attack the larger monasteries.

Some abbots had provided support for the revolt, but every monastic institution would suffer the consequences. Henry's soldiers moved into abbeys and monasteries throughout the country. Alter plates and vestments were taken to the king's jewel house, bells were melted down in the Tower of London and lead stripped from the roofs to be used as shot.

By 1537 Henry turned his attentions to the remaining religious houses. Monks were unable to leave the grounds of their buildings. Young men were no longer allowed to join religious orders. The abbeys could not survive and gradually began to close down. Brutal force was used against those who chose to resist.

The surrender of Waltham Abbey in 1540 brought the dissolution to an end. No independent religious houses remained in England, or Wales.

The surrender of Waltham Abbey

Abbey Heroes and Villains Quiz

1. In which century were the first monasteries built?
2. The 'Rule' of which Saint is observed by all monastic orders?
3. Which Saint brought Christianity to Ireland?
4. What is a 'tonsure'?
5. What did monks and nuns own?
6. In 597 AD Saint Augustine established what at Canterbury?
7. Which monastic order was the most strict and devout?
8. How many nunneries were there in Britain at the time of the Black Death?
9. Who is England's best known monastic writer?
10. How many services in one day did a monk or nun have to attend?
11. What was the name of the covered walkway where monks worked?
12. Where were the old and sick treated in a monastery?
13. Where did the Cluniac's originate from?
14. What was described as 'more fit for wild beasts to inhabit than men?
15. What did King William leave Battle Abbey?
16. What was the name of the Norman Knight who helped to rebuild Whitby Abbey?
17. Who built Jedburgh Abbey?
18. What disastrous event took place in 1184 which destroyed Glastonbury Abbey?
19. Which Saint was Llanthony Priory dedicated to?
20. True or false, in 653 AD St Aidan established the first monastery at Lindisfarne?
21. At the beginning of which century did the monastic way of life decline?
22. What was the name of the Catholic revolt against Henry VIII?
23. How did Henry VIII take his revenge on the leaders and supporters of the Catholic revolt?
24. The surrender of which abbey brought the dissolution to an end in 1540?

Answers 1. 3rd Century AD 2. The Rule of St Benedict 3. St Patrick 4. The name of the monk's distinctive haircut 5. Nothing! 6. The first Benedictine monastery. 7. Carthusian monks 8. 150 nunneries 9. The Venerable Bede 10. 7 or 8 11. Cloister 12. Infirmary 13. Cluny Abbey in France 14. The site of Fountains Abbey 15. His sword and coronation robes 16. Reinfrid 17. King David I 18. A terrible fire 19. John the Baptist 20. False - it was founded in 635 AD 21. 14th Century 22. Pilgrimage of Grace 23. He executed over 250 of them 24. Waltham Abbey